# CHRISTMAS DAY

PAUL DURCAN was born in Dublin in 1944, of County Mayo parents, and studied archaeology and medieval history at University College Cork. His first book, *Endsville* (with Brian Lynch), appeared in 1967, and has been followed by fourteen others, including *The Berlin Wall Café* (Poetry Book Society Choice, Winter 1985), *Daddy, Daddy* (Winner of the Whitbread Award for Poetry, 1990), *Crazy about Women* (1991) and *A Snail in My Prime: New and Selected Poems* (1993). Apart from Britain and Ireland, where he has read widely, he has also given readings in the former Yugoslavia, the former Soviet Union, the USA, Canada, Holland, France, Italy, Luxembourg, Belgium, New Zealand, Israel, Germany, Brazil and the Czech Republic. His most recent book is *Give Me Your Hand* (1994), a sequence of poems inspired by paintings in the National Gallery, London. He is a member of Aosdána and lives in Dublin.

D0106404

*Paul Durcan*

# CHRISTMAS DAY

with

A Goose in the Frost

THE HARVILL PRESS
LONDON

First published in Great Britain in 1996 by
The Harvill Press
84 Thornhill Road
London N1 1RD

5 7 9 10 8 6

A CIP catalogue record for this title is available from
the British Library

ISBN 978 1 86046 287 0 (hbk)
ISBN 978 1 86046 288 7 (pbk)

Designed and typeset in Minion at
Libanus Press, Marlborough, Wiltshire

Printed and bound in Great Britain by
Antony Rowe Ltd, Chippenham, Wiltshire

# CONTENTS

Christmas Day                 1

A Goose in the Frost          79

*Notes*                       88

# CHRISTMAS DAY

*For kindness it is, that ever calls forth kindness.*
SOPHOCLES

*No longer are you to be named 'Forsaken',*
*nor your land 'Abandoned',*
*but you shall be called 'My Delight'*
*and your land 'The Wedded'.*

I

The day after St Stephen's Day
Frank telephoned me at 10.30 a.m.:
'I am sorry about the Christmas crackers, Paul,
I clean forgot all about the Christmas crackers.

I got up this morning at 6 a.m., Paul,
When I remembered about the Christmas crackers.
I had breakfast in the airport cafeteria.
I appeared to be the only man on the escalator.

Women arriving, women departing.
When you saw that I had no Christmas crackers
Why didn't you say something?
You are too polite for your own good.

I had coffee and crispies
Sitting opposite a civil servant from Dolphin's Barn.
She is going away to the Andes
With the Friends of Kew Gardens.'

'But Frank, you had balloons.
I adored your balloons.
To hell with crackers.
Balloons are what matter.'

II

Christmas Day
I spend alone
In my cave
Rotating my globe
Musing what it would be like
To spend Christmas Day
With another human being
Or what it would be like
To spend Christmas Day
In New Zealand –
Biting the light
In Timaru –
Or listening to my solitary
Schubert cassette,
Radu Lupu
Playing *Moments Musicaux*,
Replaying the cassette
Again and again
To drown out neighbour-noise
But also for its own noise,
Its oblivion-honey
That I want never
To stop guzzling at
Or rereading
My favourite novel
*A Farewell to Arms*
Or my favourite biography
*John XXXIII*
Or browsing
In rhyme –

In Gunn
Or Housman –
But this year
My pal Frank
Invited me in the afternoon
Up to his top-storey flat
In a new apartment block
In Terenure,
On the Rathfarnham Road,
Behind the *Sunday World*,
In the southern suburbs
Of Dublin city,
On the outskirts of the foothills
Of the Dublin mountains.

This was a simple arrangement.
No complications.
Not like having to decide
Not whether to go to Mass
But which Mass to attend:
Vigil Mass? Night Mass?
Early Morning Mass? Day Mass?
Which would it be?
Which should it be?
Which could it be?
Horizontal in bed
I ran rings round my toes
Trying to make the right choice.
In the event, I solved the problem
By deciding not to go to any Mass.
What would Frank say?
Who on an August night

On Dollymount strand,
Watching the sea
Typing up its tidings –
A hare in the headlights –
Delved with such perky innocence,
Such blue-eyed curiosity,
Are you a practising Catholic?
That I did not squirm.
I had no qualm
In disclosing with gusto – Yes.
A *practising* Catholic!
I practise and practise and practise
And, when I get the chance, I play.

I keep beads
On my bedside table
That I got in Jerusalem
In the Arab quarter.
Worry beads.
In my bedside drawer
I keep my father's rosary beads
Which along with *Palgrave's
Golden Treasury*
Were all that he had
When he died demented,
Alone and palely raving.
I like the feel of beads.
If you haven't got earrings –
And I haven't because I've no one
To tell me how to put them on or in –
Beads are the thing to have.
I like bowing;

I've nothing against genuflection
But I prefer bowing.
I like blessing myself;
Dipping my fingers in water;
Fonts,
But ideally
Rainwater butts.
I cannot pass a church
Without blessing myself.
On aircraft at takeoff and landing
I make the sign of the cross
And gabble the Our Father.
At all times of the day
I gabble the Our Father
Stumbling as always on
'Forgive us our trespasses
As we forgive those who trespass against us.'
But, as Frank says,
Because you forgive them
Does not mean you have to like them.
I say the Our Father when I drive
Past the cemetery where my father
Crawled into the oven –
His emaciated ankles sprouting smoke.
In cities across the world
I like sitting in churches doing nothing.
I like going to communion:
Standing in line and catching
Glimpses in night skies
Through x-rays of clouds
Of the thin white moon of the host.
The moment I took the decision

Not to go to Mass
I could feel life returning into my body,
My empty cistern filling up,
The Holy Spirit gurgling inside me.

I should do this more often –
Not go to Mass.
It is difficult not to go to Mass.
Mass is the only chance
One has to be in company,
To be in society.
To emit.
I do not mean to meet
People, I mean simply to be
With and among people;
To be in the real presence
Of people other than oneself.
To be choral.
Dumb is nobody.

The skin on my face
Is beige and my hair is grey
From woman-hunger.
For days the phone
Does not ring and then
When it does and I run
To snatch it up
The shy, reticent voice
Of a woman in the South Island,
New Zealand, whispers
'I'd like to knit you a woolly hat
But I don't know

What is between those ears of yours.'
To live alone
Is not to know
One day from the next:
Letting myself in
And out of the house;
Tramping the streets
With my skull on my neck
And with my hand in my pocket
Twiddling my house key.
Christmas is the Feast of St Loneliness.
I street-walk at night
Looking in the windows
Of other people's houses
Assessing their Christmas decorations,
Marking them out of ten.
This Christmas I have spotted
In the front window of a three-storey
Town house in Percy Place
A little Christmas tree
Adorned only
With electric candles.
I give it eight out of ten.
What amazes me this Christmas
Is all the menorahs.
Menorahs are all the craze.
Every second window in Ringsend
Has a menorah. Oh, Sharon,
Your menorah is only gorgeous.
Don't be talking, Deborah.

\*

Although the Church has come
To the end of its historical life
I am loath
To abandon the sinking ship.
Who could have foreseen
At early morning Mass
In the winter of 1956 –
Serving Father Ned Keane,
Sniffing the bloom of altar wine,
Rattling the bells for the sanctus,
My long pants showing underneath my soutane
Tagged with bicycle clips,
My bicycle pump in my jacket pocket,
My bicycle lamp on the altar step,
*Ad deum qui laetificat juventutem meam* –
That we would live to see
The Church sink in our lifetime?
Not Gerry Owens and me –
Two eleven-year-old altar boys
Cycling home in the dark
From early morning Mass;
Two heads racing the dawn,
Glued to dropped handlebars;
Our eyes on the Tour de France,
On crashing traffic lights.
Not even in the snowy gloom
Of the winter of 1981 –
In the Polish Seminary in Paris,
Reeking of urine,
Where I perched for a year
In a cell on the third floor
In black – not

To have to wash –
And the Polish Rector greeted me
On the stairs every morning
'Bonjour, mon père' –
Did anyone discern
Icebergs looming
– Poised at angles –
Fore and aft the Church.
The Polish concierge
Cupped my face in his claws;
His fingernails were uncut black;
He squawked, Knock!
For the first time in my forty-nine-year-old life
On Christmas Day
I did not go to Mass.
Instead I stayed in bed and listened
On my Walkman to the Eucharist Service
Broadcast from St Nicholas's Collegiate Church
      in Galway:
Hymn No. 60 and a minister
From Northern Ireland preaching
A sermon about what he called
'The magic of reality'.

In the bosom of loneliness
I sit up in bed in my headphones
Watching the black rain
Flaking away at my window,
Chiselling at my double-glaze –
Swarms of chisel points;
The faces of my daughters
Picked out in raindrops;

Their scrubbed, drowned, peeling,
Fresco faces;
The faces of friends:
Francis Stuart at ninety-three
In his yellow bungalow
In Dundrum
On the banks of the River Slang
After falling on the back-garden steps
Half-sitting up in his bed
In the corner of his bare bedroom,
Snowed under by floorboards,
All alone in the universe,
Chuckling that he wants for nothing
Except a cup of tea.
From the shores of his bedclothes
He looks out at me, waving.
Derek Mahon
Peering out at me
From behind his spectacles
At the back of the Xtra-Vision
Video Store in Baggot Street
At 3.15 p.m.
In the dark of an early January
Afternoon and *pianissimo*
Lighting up the dark
With the phosphorus of recognition
And the teeth of his laughter.
'If you want to order *Dracula*,'
The video storeman enlightens him,
'I will need your credit card number.'
Colm Tóibín shivering on the platform
Of Swansea railway station

On a cold March morning
Looks up from his *Guardian*:
'Did you know Gerard Victory?
Gerard Victory is dead.'
When I hear the minister's voice
(Or is it a priest's voice? Have I
Got my wavelengths mixed up?)
Beseeching over the air waves,
On the astra satellite from Ireland,
'Let us offer one another the Sign of Peace'
I know that if I slid out of bed,
Tripped downstairs in my dressing gown
Out onto the street,
Knocked on the neighbour's door,
Offered him the Sign of Peace,
He'd grunt 'Hump off'.
At Holy Communion
I pour hot coffee from my flask –
Bewley's Medium Roast For Filters –
Into my mug inscribed PAUL.
It was a nun in Rome
Gave me a mug with my name.
I swallow it with my eyes closed.
'Do this in commemoration of me.'

III

'Smashing flat –'
I mutter as Frank takes my red scarf
And my overcoat –
The blue gaberdine
From Marks and Spencer's;
My black galoshes
That were my father's galoshes;
'Much as I would like to die in my galoshes
I'd rather you had my galoshes.
If you will take good care of my galoshes
You may have my galoshes.
The right galosh has a new sole.
The left galosh has a new upper.'
I had no designs on my father's galoshes
But with his golf clubs at his feet
And with his galoshes in his hands –
Waving with his galoshes at me,
Flicking his galoshes at mc,
Pucking me in the gob with his galoshes,
Procuring me with his galoshes
To dance a jig on my ego –
My father cornered me in the Playroom –
The Playroom that used be the Maid's Room
And that was ordained to become the Sun Room
But declined to become the Sun Room
Because it was facing north –
The Playroom where I used play trains
On my hands and knees
With Reggie MacMahon –
And rather than have a debate

And find myself postulating a universe
In which instead of the Playroom,
The Sun Room, the Pantry, the Study, the Passage,
There are only rooms
With wainscots, nettles,
Only nouns
Without definite articles,
I took the galoshes, put on the galoshes,
Walked off lopsidedly in the galoshes,
Staggered off home in the galoshes
Down the Grand Canal,
Across Grand Canal Street
Past Kitty O'Shea's
And Estate Cottages
Into the Ringsend sector.
My red scarf
That I got in Kevin and Howlin's
1984 New Year Sale,
One of three red scarves
I bought in that sale.
I gave one to Frank
After I came home
From Moscow in 1986.
Frank wore it for five years
Boasting in good faith
To all the *boulevardiers*
In Harry Street
His Russian scarf!
He sucks in his cheeks,
Lets a roar out of the side of his mouth:
'I am a penthouse man now
And ever will be.'

We guffaw. He puffs:
'Paul, come into the parlour,
Make yourself at home.
Who killed Rob Roy?
Welcome to the James
Robertson Justice
Cat Doctors Society.
After paws and purrs
Glynis Johns
Will take you to her bosoms.
O Holy Valley!
If you're a bonny boy
Billy Panama will give you a go
On his yo-yo.
Bonny boys are few.
Comes ins, comes ins.'

He invited me out of the blue
A week ago
The day I drove him down
In the snow
To visit his mother in Jericho –
A hospice where old people
Subsist with a soupçon of dignity
As they queue up for the final curtain,
An oasis in the desert.
Over the hills
And far away
In County Wicklow.
How many curtains to Jericho?

*

I step across the open suitcase
Beside the empty drinks cupboard:
Shirts, pullovers, shoelaces,
Earplugs, pastilles, combs, vitamins,
Elastoplast, batteries, disposable blades,
Condoms, biros, memo pads,
Creams, rubber bands, luggage labels.
'I was working in Milan, Paul,
With a guy called Coyote Shivers.
Had supper every other night
With him in the trattoria.
Pass me the salt, Coyote.
Pass me the bread, Coyote.
Good night, Coyote.
A man of saliva.
Liked to look the waiter
In the eye and drawl
'My name is Coyote Shivers.
I'm thinking of marrying your mother.'
Many nights that's all he'd say:
'My name is Coyote Shivers.
I'm thinking of marrying your mother.'

I am staring at the empty drinks cupboard.
Frank notices me.
'Isn't that a scenic spectacle, Paul?
More scenic than a full drinks cupboard,
More soul-enticing.'
'Don't I know, Frank,
The vanishing splendour – isn't that the name
Of a pub in Notting Hill Gate?'
'The Sun in Splendour.'

'The Sun in Splendour –
The vanishing splendour
Of the full drinks cupboard.
All those Christmasses in Cork
And the six week lead-ups
When every other night on the way home
From work in the rain, I'd stop off
At Galvin's Off-Licence on the Bandon Road
And select a different bottle of spirits:
A Vision of Christmas
As the Nativity of Alcohol;
All the churches stacked
Floor to ceiling
With crates of liquor;
Archangels of whiskey, gin, vodka,
Brandy, lager, stout, wine,
Vermouth, crème de menthe,
Sherry, port, rum, martini,
Campari, Angostura bitters –
I was a blackguard for the campari –
And a copy from Eason's
Of *Teach Yourself Christmas Cocktails*
Or – imported from Stateside –
*Screwballs For Avantgarde Housewives*.
On Christmas Day I'd say
Mass alone in my private chapel;
Kneel alone at my own
Prie-dieu at the crib,
Opening bottle after bottle,
Lighting candles, delighting
In darkness, retiring to bed
At five in the afternoon with the paperback

Edition of the new life of Roger
Casement by Brian Inglis, giving
Thanks to God for the invention
Of the bottle opener and the corkscrew.
Where would man be
Without the opposable thumb?
It's bad enough man
Not having a tail.
Next morning, St Stephen's Day,
The serratedly red-eyed
Hungover next-door neighbour
Rattling on my front door
To ask if he may park
His crashed car –
Leatherette seats shredded
With shattered glass –
In our front garden
And when I demur
His four-year-old son
Starts to bark and
Bites me on the wrist.
Frank, your empty drinks cupboard
Placates my eyes.'

I pace up and down.
'Paul, do you like my balloons?
Blue for the bathroom,
Red for the bedroom,
Green for the parlour,
Yellow for the kitchen.'
'I like your balloons, Frank.
Do you know what a woman

– She was being candid,
Confidential, conjugal –
Whispered to me
Over her shoulder
Across her buttock
In the middle of the night?
"You're like a burst balloon!"'
'What could you say to that?
Dear God!
Confrontations on rooftops
In the middle of the night.
We're all white men in Ireland, Paul.
That is the problem.
The women are fed up to their tusks
Seeing nothing but white men.
White men, white men.
For 10,000 years in Dublin –
60,000 years in Dublin –
Nothing but white men.
It's not realistic.
White men in white underwear
Or, which is the crux of the conundrum,
Off-white men in off-white underwear.
Is there anything more calculated to deflate
Than the sight of yourself in the looking glass
In a pair of yellowing long johns?
Yesterday I put on a pair of black briefs
Over my white long johns
But to tell you the truth I looked disgraceful.
I am fed up
Seeing nothing but white women

In O'Connell Street and Grafton Street.
I sit in Bewley's Oriental Café
In Grafton Street –
Pete Short feeding birds at the door –
Pete Short must spend a fortune
On birdfood! –
With a pencil sharpener
In my hand in my pocket
Praying for a black woman
To pour through the door
And flood me out;
To be up to my knees in black women;
To be two-and-a-half feet
Deep in black women;
Lying awake in bed at night
Yearning for black women
I am a pine tree
Creaking in a gale,
I am a steamer in a storm
Groaning on the ocean.
But in thirty years not one
Black woman have I seen
In Dublin.
Although I am not the marrying kind
I'd have married years ago
If there'd been black women in Dublin.
Black and white –
My favourite colours.
Waking up in the morning and finding
A black face on the pillow
Beside me and a black arm

Across my white stomach.
The Ma would have enjoyed
A black daughter-in-law.
A white one would have bored her.'

'Black or white, Frank –
A woman in whose drift
To get bogged down.
I wouldn't mind if a woman was an
Anglo-Saxon Aromatherapist in Arizona
So long as I could get
Bogged down in her drift.'
His inviting me out of the blue
Was a shock to the system.
I expected him to say
'If I don't see you *before* Christmas Day,
I'll see you *after* Christmas Day.'
Instead I hear him say
En route to Jericho
As we turn left for Kilbride
'Come up Christmas Day.'
Kilbride before Blessington
Where his oldest friends
Live under the mountain,
Under Kippure:
A retired British Army officer
Who towards the end of the war
Fell in love in Palermo
With an Italian princess
And made her his batman
And after the war his wife.
Frank sighs as we throb

Through the snow,
The dirty-black snow
Under the mountain:
'Not like me in Budapest
When I was there on my first job
Almost exactly thirty years ago.
They sent me down
One weekend to Bulgaria.
At a party in Sofia
I met a Bulgarian woman,
A Bulgar dame,
Twenty-two years old,
The true Mediterranean type,
The kind of woman in whom
Femininity is a principle –
A conflagration
Which flames out of every pore of her
And does not expire with age.
Like Sophia Loren or
Gina Lollobrigida.
Tease me, if you like.
Although she did not speak
A word of English
Nor I a word of Bulgarian
We clicked on the spot.
A stroke of tenderness!
On the Monday morning
I went back to Budapest –
Pest was my billet
But I was based in Buda –
And learned Bulgarian.
We wrote thousands of letters

And postcards to one another.
But I never met her again
Except once when her train
From Sophia to East Berlin
Was passing through Budapest.
I was waiting for her
Three days in the railway station.
Which train would she be on?
Which platform would she arrive at?
I saw her face in the window.
A teardrop on her cheekbone.
We had an hour on the train
In the corridor outside her
Full-up compartment.
Never saw her again.
She got married in East Berlin
To a Chilean Communist.
After the 1973 coup in Chile –
The overthrow of Allende –
She disappeared. Last Christmas –
Twenty-nine years since we met –
She sent me a Christmas card.
She's divorced and living in Ecuador.
A bank clerk in Quito.'

'Close to the bone, Frank.'
'Will I put another log on the fire, Paul?
Great yokes – logs.
When did you last *smell* log-smoke?
When did you last *see* log-smoke?
The trick is to put on one log at a time
And not to stoke it. No flames.

I can live without flames.
Much as I hanker after flames
Flames can burn you out of house and home.
What do you think of my candles?
I lit the candle in the hallway
While you were ascending the elevator.
You were a long time ascending.
Could you hear me on the intercom?
I'll blow it out now and light it again
When the Bowler arrives. No point
In letting good candlelight go to waste.'

IV

Frank is in the kitchen
Cooking Christmas Dinner
For himself and myself.
He and I for Christmas Dinner.
'Are you in good voice, Paul?
Your speaking-in-public voice?
Chant me a new anthem.'
I demur but Frank insists.
I chant him a new anthem –
'An Item Once Again':

> *An item once again!*
> *An item once again!*
> *If you promise me you'll laugh all day,*
> *You can have me for your birthday.*

> I met her on my birthday
> In the Berkeley Court Hotel;
> She sat me down and slapped my face
> And said, Well, now, are you well?
> You're only fifty years of age
> And I am over thirty;
> If you promise me you'll laugh all day
> You can have me for your birthday.

> *An item once again!*
> *An item once again!*
> *If you promise me you'll laugh all day,*
> *You can have me for your birthday.*

Frank brandishes a casserole dish:
'Good man, Paul, y'old snail you.'
'Can I do anything in the kitchen, Frank?'
'You can not. Keep out of the kitchen
Or I'll kill you.
Would you like an appetizer, Paul?
Smoked salmon and brown bread?'
I pluck a piece but, clown that I am,
Omit to discern the half-moon of lemon.
Frank makes it clear
That he is not prepared to condone
This sort of behaviour on Christmas afternoon.
'Paul, you're not in New Zealand now:
Squeeze your lemon.'
Frank knows all, or a lot,
About me and New Zealand:
Broken toes in Basin Reserve;
Broken ribs in Eden Park.

I spot the *Sunday Independent* on the floor
Between the television set and the couch.
Today – Christmas Day – is Saturday.
The *Sunday Independent* came out yesterday, Friday.
Man can bend himself to anything.
I sound like an Old Testament prophet.
One can if one talks to oneself.
If one talks to oneself for long enough
In the bath – if one has a bath. I haven't.
My dream is to have a bath.
Water to lie in
As well as to stand in.
I don't buy newspapers

Except for the *RTE Guide*
Which comes out on a Wednesday;
I read through the programmes for the coming week,
Ringing my selections with a red Bic biro.
Water to soak in
Mermaid-like awhile
Listening to the ads on the wireless:
Brendan Kennelly, in his Kerry
Sports commentator voice,
Wooing us
To read the *Sunday Independent*;
John Kavanagh in bardic mode
Intoning an ode to Bulmer's Cider;
Donal McCann with his chest to his cards –
'There is still life with Ballygowan.'
Frank is roaring at me from the kitchen:
'Did you ever smell another man's seed?
I did in the cell of the cop shop in Blessington.
Another man's seed-stains
On the cell blanket. Grey issue.
Naught for it but to shag blanket on floor.
I made do without it but it was terrible cold.
Would you care for a mug of celery soup?'

He ladles me out a mug of celery soup.
Am I losing my marbles?
I had not realized how sad
And silent I am
Until this Christmas afternoon.
Suddenly I am shocked
By the spectacle of myself –
A forty-nine-year-old male with little

Or nothing to say:
Too sad to utter.
When I do utter, I utter
In a stutter:
'F – F – Frank.'
I woke up this morning
Unable to speak
For fear that the gas-boiler
Vibrating over my bed
Would explode.
The knife of woman-hunger
Has diluted me.
Physically I am standing here
In Frank's kitchen, vertical.
Mentally I am flat on the lino,
Eked out, stutter-spliced.

'Before I went out to Brazil, Frank,
I telephoned the Department of Foreign Affairs
To check which Irish Embassy
Represents Ireland in Brazil.
But I could not say "Brazil".
The word would not squeeze out.
Not even the "B". Especially not the "B".
"I am travelling to . . . excuse me."
I had to hang up.
I rang back ten minutes later
Running my words together
In a Dublin accent,
My chest detonating.
"I'm goin' workin' in –
In – in – in – in –

Brazil next week."
Choked. Scalded.
I knew she knew it was me.
In a jaded, bland, bumptious voice
She informed me that she did not know
Which Irish Embassy
Represents Ireland in Brazil.
She yawned,
"Try Portugal."
Consider being up the creek
In the Amazon and having to stammer
To the local Indians
Brandishing their mobiles
That because I am Irish
To t – t – t – t – t –
Try Portugal.

But Brazil was good to me –
Two B's there for you! –
And when I got home,
Outside Glasnevin Crematorium,
At Tiernan MacBride's funeral
After being sniffed at
By breeches in ponchos,
I was greeted by Peter Sheridan:
"You are one of life's travellers."
Strange to say!
But it's true.
Every year I travel far away
In search of the Abominable Snowman –
That is to say, the Abominable Woman.
Why? Why the Abominable Woman?

Because she is all
That is delicate, courteous, cordial.
I have caught glimpses of her
In Jerusalem, Dunedin, Rio de Janeiro,
But only once in ten years
Have I actually met her –
In Rossnaree
On the banks of the Boyne
On the towpath at twilight
Gazing across the river
At Egypt and Newgrange,
All those flocks and herds
Of sheep and camels,
The pyramids and the shepherds,
The lone coach-driver
Waving goodbye to the tour guide
Locking up for the night –
She who is – I do not know her Christian name –
Mimi La Touche's second eldest daughter –
All that is delicate, courteous, cordial.
Not a death-to-all-men woman –
Not on a good day
When she lets her hair down
And she sits up in bed
Late into the night combing it
While she dictates to me
And we chat, prick, dilate
And sitting on the stairs
I read aloud to her
*The Duino Elegies*
And the black cat escapes.

*

Upstream at midnight
Under a full moon
She is engraved in the ruins
Of a Cistercian Abbey
In long black coat
And long grey skirt
At home in the universe.
The car headlights
Spoon her in the neck,
The moonlight forks her hair,
Her profile in silhouette.
She chides me
As she has always chided me:
"Don't run after the cat;
All you need do is call it."
It is not possible for a woman
To be patient with a man.
He cannot be loved;
Therefore, he does not exist.
All she can hope to do
Is to ameliorate her dismay.
While she plants trees at the source
He is compelled to talk.
On and on he talks of the physiology of rivers
And wrecks at the bar
While at the source she is planting trees –
Japanese Cypress, Monterey Pine,
Incense Cedar, Golden Yew.
He believes in God – in saying words;
She does not believe in God –
She believes in planting trees;

The Abominable Woman who is all
That is delicate, courteous, cordial.

One of life's travellers!
Hailed also as "The Tinker Durcan"
When I was walking across
The Green in Castlebar
In the summer of 1988
After my father had died
And I was missing him.
On both sides of my family
We were all Tinkers
And Protestants – Protestant Tinkers.
And that was okay until the big guns
Of the family became Settled Catholics
And there was hell to pay
If you were a little gun like me
Who wanted to stay a Protestant Tinker.
In any pink-and-grey case
That's what I've been all my life
From Copacabana to Portballantrae,
A Protestant Tinker.'

## V

I crouch back up on the edge
Of the black leather upholstered couch,
Assemble myself – my ankles
Sore, my gums stinging,
My green underpants inclining
To sag, to fall
Down, their elasticity gone –
Gaze up into the Van Gogh print over the
    fireplace:
*Rooftops in Auvers-sur-Oise.*
Down in the lobby of the apartment block
I was startled by a Picasso print.
The little punk girl with the dove.
The TV has a BBC2 documentary on the life of
    a star –
'The Star in the East' roars Frank from the kitchen.
Geological as well as theological data.
Followed by a documentary on dolphins:
'Dolphins are a threatened species.'
Frank roars: 'Aren't we all?'
'What?'
'Threatened.'
'By whom?'
'By man.'
Frank looms in the doorway
With whetstone and carving knife
In a Beatrix Potter apron:
Mr Frog.
As gradually he sharpens the knife,
Gradually he loses his temper.

'Do you see the Three Rock Mountain
Outside my window?
A sleepy little mountain
That never hurt a fly
And with whom I played
And you played and we all played
In High Infants-Prep School time;
Who gave us rides on his back
Every Sunday afternoon
1948 to 1958.
Well now, that same
Sleepy little mountain
Has Aids but shucks,
Nobody is supposed to say so
In case one might have to
Do something about it,
Like recycle our garbage
Or use leadfree fuel.
What's a fucking mountain?
There is not a mountain,
Lake or river in Ireland,
Not a bog or a callow,
That does not have Aids.
Where be your corncrakes now?
Your hay? Your elm tree?'
Frank smiles: 'The turkey is at tongue temperature.'
He will not let me carry in a plate.
(Afterwards he will not let me do the washing up.)
'Creamed potatoes, ham, Brussels sprouts
And five roast potatoes especially for Paul
And bags of stuffing especially for Paul
And cranberry sauce that I made myself.'

# VI

Frank is proud of himself.
I am proud of Frank.
He has not only prepared the feast
But he has set the table.
The set table
Which is the city of God
According to Manuel Bandeira
In Santa Teresa,
Rio de Janeiro.
Napkins
& skyscrapers.
Condiments
& flyovers.
Frank says grace:
'He hath showed thee, O man,
What is good;
And what does the Lord require of thee
But to do justly, and to love mercy,
And to walk humbly with thy God.'
In the middle of the table
Centre-stage
Perches a miniature Christmas Tree –
Plastic –
With a candle inside it.
In silence we stare at it –
At the minuscule flame of candlelight flickering
With all around it the black lacy tide foaming in –
Our four eyes peering at the embryo of flame
As well as at each last penultimate wave breaking –

All these peregrinations and perambulations
    of peripheries.
Frank whispers: 'Where is my cigarette lighter?'
With a cigarette – Silk Cut
(He is trying to stay off
The Benson & Hedges)
Dangling from the corner of his mouth
He dotes on all this food and plenty
Which he – and he alone –
Has put on the table.
He proclaims: 'Lash into it.'

We run around the table,
Flap our wings, get down
Into low chairs. Our Adam's apples
Chug into port. Two turkeys
Sitting down to Christmas Dinner
In excitement, yet grief,
Mindful of our case histories –
The Turkey Sheds
That so many of our contemporaries
Did not survive.
Two-faced padlocks.
In wet twilight
All those thousands of pink gobs
Black with fright.
I'm a turkey who'd settle
For a mobile home in a field
Of milk cattle
With the wireless only for company:
Shostakovich's *Leningrad Symphony*

Or Christy Moore
'North and South of the River'
Or Oonagh Keogh
'The 24th Paganini Caprice'
Or Ben Webster moaning on tenor sax
With Ella Fitzgerald
'In a Mellow Tone'.
I have always thought
Since one night in the bath
In Lower Montenotte in 1976 –
We had a bath in Lower Montenotte –
In fact, we lived
In a house in Lower Montenotte –
That if I was a poet
Billy Strayhorn would be the poet
I'd emulate.
Or Basil Blackshaw:
To learn how to mix
Defiance and caution
In equal proportion;
The Brigitte Bardot poster on the door
Beside Mont Sainte-Victoire.
Poetry's another word
For losing everything
Except purity of heart.
In my mobile home on the hill
I'd hang my aerial out of the beech tree
And fill up my breeze blocks
And my rubber tyres
With sunflowers and gnomes,
Gladioli and foxglove,
And be a martyr to

Sunday mornings in bed –
*Desert Island Discs*
Created and devised by Roy Plumley;
*Mo Cheol Thú*
And *Sunday Miscellany;*
Ronnie Walsh spilling
Milk into saucers
For kittens and crooning the praises
Of light music;
Ciarán Mac Mathúna collecting
The eggs and murmuring
'The Humours of Donnybrook';
John Jordan slicing
Onions and declaiming
'An *hommage* to Edith Piaf';
Seamus Ennis on the uillean pipes
Under the bird feeder on the drainpipe
Clawing 'Easter Snow'.

We are hungry. We eat in silence.
Except for me stuttering:
'I – I – I – I visited my father's grave
In Glasnevin Cemetery at midday.
Well, grave is not the word.
His name is on a plaque
Along with fifty-nine other names:
George N. Pillow, Leilah Bolton,
Rose Duff, Gladys Lucas,
Geoffrey Swain, John J. Durcan.
Good Protestant names.
Euphony. Cremated.
But where are the ashes?

I have not an iota.
John Arlott, how are ye!
The inscription under the plaque states:

> NO MONUMENTS, NO FLOWERPOTS
>
> OR OTHER MEMORIALS
>
> SHALL BE PERMITTED IN
>
> THE VICINITY OF THE
>
> GARDEN OF REMEMBRANCE

I took out my notebook and biro,
Scrawled DADDY on ten separate pages,
Tore out and scattered them in the vicinity
Of the Garden of Remembrance.
I took courage from the crowds.
All that sellotape!
All those scissors!
It was like being in a cemetery
In Moscow on a Sunday afternoon.
Such crowds on Christmas Day!
Such masses of flowers!
Vaganskoye! Novodevichy!
All the Foleys, all the O'Tooles.
All the Vysostskys, all the Ivinskayas.'
Frank reins me in with a kick of his smile:
'Paul, you and I are two Russians.'
'True enough, I suppose, Frank.'
'Paul, to put a long tooth in it,
A pair of Dostoyevskys
Or, would you say, Dostoys?
A right pair of Dostoys.
Old Believers.
Grasshoppers. Crickets.
Not Irishmen.

Definitely not Irishmen.
Dubliners. With roots
In the mountains and the lakes.
Two men of no property.
Do men rate
Who have no real estate?
On an apple-ripe September morning
In the public library in Invercargill
I sauntered through fields that were part
Of no literary estate.
Will you have the plum pudding now or later,
　　Paul?'
'I'll wait a bit if you don't mind, Máire.'
'I don't mind, Paul, I don't mind one little bit
But I have a confession to make – it's packet
　　plum pudding.
Only – I am not Máire, I am Frank.'
'Frank. Sorry Frank. Frank.'
'Don't be sorry, Paul. Whatever else
Don't be sorry or you might be sorry.
I don't think of my father
Down in the dead leaves.
I don't visit my father's grave.
I don't know where my father's grave is.
I think of my father running for the bus
On winter mornings in the 1950s.
He used time the run
From the hall door to the moving platform;
Hat, umbrella, newspaper;
He'd sprint from door to platform;
Hop, step and jump; land
With his arm around the vertical rail;

Wave to my ma in the porch.
Timing is what's next to godliness.
My da was a godly man.
Tea or coffee, Mr D?'
'I'm all right, Frank.'
'For the love of Scobie, Paul,
Will you stop being so polite –
It does not become you.
The horriblest git in Ireland
Is that murderous little archimatect,
Carleton O'Flaherty.
We are agreed on that.
That baldy little satyr
From Mulhuddart, ensconced
In his solar pad in Shrewsbury Road
With his two Doberman Pinschers
And his five wives
Who all went to Mount Anville.
*We all went to Mount Anville*
You can hear them screeching
From the rooftops of Shrewsbury Road.
*We all went to Mount Anville*
*And took a degree in sociology*
*In UCD.*
You could do with a little
Murder in your soul, Paul.
Now, you can have any kind
Of coffee your intestines crave:
Maxwell House Instantaneous
Or Bewley's Groundswoman –
I do a mischievous
Blend of slinky Costa Rica

And husky French Roast –
Or you can have chaste Barry's Tea
Or Early Grey
Or Tardy Breakfast
Or even Breaking Orange Pekoe
Or Twig Smithereens.'
'I'll have a cup of hot water.'
'By the hokey, Mr D,
You are an exotic creature.'
When I fish out from my breast pocket
A teabag of herbal –
Rose Hip –
And slip it
Into the cup of hot water
Frank raises his eyebrows
Higher than I have seen
Anyone's eyebrows ever go –
So high I begin to see
His eyebrows scuttling about
The wainscotting of his scalp
Between his forehead and hairline.
When I scoop out the teabag
And drop it in the ashtray –
An Eiffel Tower ashtray from Paris –
He snatches it and holds it up
To the light like a mad cat
With a mouse by the tail,
His eyes all teeth a-glittery;
Swinging my teabag
By its limp G-string;
'What have we got here?'
After a brief, hot struggle

With my anger and shame,
My whining *amour propre*,
I see that he is not a catatonic cat
But a fifty-year-old child
Luxuriating in astoundment –
He has never before in his life seen
A herbal tea-drinking male of the species.
'Rose Hip – you don't tell me!'
He murmurs over and over
Like Lord Tennyson making love
To his chambermaid – 'Rose Hip!'

While Frank remains rapt in Rose
Hip, oscillating
Sump to and fro
In a reverie of thurible-
Swinging in a harem –
Moaning '*Infusing, infusing*' –
My eyes orbit him speaking to themselves:
There was a young widow in black
In Glasnevin Cemetery. I heard her
Before I saw her – the tapping
On the tarmacadam of her high heels.
I spun around and I saw her
Hurdling towards me across the headstones,
Her yellow hair tucked into her black suede jacket,
Her blue mini-skirt more daring than a fig leaf,
The white ponies of her teeth
Riding red lipstick.
As we were about to pass
We stopped and stared
And she smiled and I gazed

Into the waterfall of her eyes
Waiting for it to stop
Thinking that she was a clock
But she was not a clock –
She was a woman,
A preoccupied soul.
Is there a role
For my twenty-three-year-old son?
She said: 'Have you got the time?'
I said: 'It is three o'clock.'
She said – as if I had invented time –
With dismay: 'Is it three o'clock?'
And I wanted to change my mind and say
That there was no time today,
That Christmas Day is a timeless day.
Instead I repeated: 'It is three o'clock'
And she walked on out of my life
Up the aisle under the yews
Towards the Parnell altar stone.
When she was out of earshot I said to her:
'May I hold your hand?'

VII

Back down into the black leather upholstery
And George C. Scott with a beard in khaki
Explaining, defending, preserving dolphins.
I deposit my Christmas present for Frank
On his chair hoping he won't sit on it.
Gift-wrapped in a cheap sheet of ruddy Santa Clauses.
(Five sheets for 50p in Moore Street
On the night before Christmas Eve.)
Frank roars: 'Time for exchange of presents, is it?'
Chuckling, he claws at my present
But it is all too obvious it comprises a book.
He reads out the title: *Soho Square 6.*
He grins, slams it shut, puts it under his chair,
Stands up, bends down over fireplace,
Plucks up a large package.
Impossible to guess what is inside it.

Frank's Christmas present to me
Is a pair of AA Driving Gloves
'Suitable' the logo says 'For Both Men & Women'
And a Cockpit Kit – Clock, Compass and
        Thermometer –
And a Christmas card made by himself.
'Oh Frank, you thoughtful man, thank you.'
'My pleasure, Paul, my pleasure.
It is mandatory – is that the word? –
To honour your accomplishment
In having learned to drive a motoring car at
        forty-nine
And to having passed your test first time out.

Don't take offence but I did not expect
You to pass your driving test,
Certainly not first time out.
Two Christmases ago
Do you remember what you said to me?
"Don't tell anyone
But I am taking driving lessons."
I was amazed when I heard you'd passed.'
'I was amazed myself, Frank.
After the test, as we walked from the car
Into the centre, the tester said to me:
"You are a natural driver, Mr Durcan."
"No, I'm not" I'd like to have said.
Instead I said "Thank you" and blushed.
There is no such thing as a natural driver
Or a natural golfer or a natural poet.
In the six months prior to the test
I spent hundreds of hours
On dull, grey, empty, Sunday afternoons
Practising on the driving-test course –
Practising, practising –
The streets of Navan town.
The streets of Navan town are a trial.'

I am too timid to try on the gloves in front of
        the fireplace.
Later tonight I will try them out in bed.
Soft leather palms, polyester backs.
Visions of Paul
'Juan Fangio' Durcan
Driving round Ireland
For the sake of it –

And for nothing else.
I only like doing a thing
For the sake of it.
I am bejasus banjaxed
If it's for a reason.
Taking a vagary and
Motoring down to Westport
And calling in on Mary MacBride
In the Old Rectory
And taking the kids out for a spin,
All five of them,
Bernardine, Erc, Una,
Síabhra, Mary Catherine,
Showing off to them,
Sliding back the sun roof,
Changing gears with the backs of my hands,
Caressing the steering wheel –
Paying it out like rosary beads –
Cuddling my car phone
To phone up Marian Finucane
On her radio programme,
*Liveline*,
Putting a Van Morrison tape
Into the cassette, turning
Up the volume to full,
'No guru, no method, no teacher'
Or 'Among those rolling hills',
Hitting the back road
To Leenane and turning off
For Tourmakeady and stopping
On the side of a mountain to see
Who can hear a bell-wether

In the flock or to listen
To Big Dermot Seymour
Leaning on a six-barred gate
Taking a raincheck on the EEC
Or the coast road to Killadoon,
Lislongley, Rathviney,
Out past Rosbeg, Mallow Cottage,
Sunnyside, Lecanvey, Murrisk,
Dropping the kids back
After ice creams at the Quay –
Three 99s and two 40s –
And being asked to stay to tea
And to meet George Birmingham,
Not the politician,
And Monsignor Dominick of Knock
In charge of the apparition
And Mr Low the radiologist
From Bloemfontein
In Castlebar doing a locum
Whose father forty years ago,
After failing to thrash poetry
Into his son, roared:
'You are not my son.'
I gaze into Frank's Christmas card.
It is a colour photo taken by himself
In – above all places –
A penthouse in Manhattan
Of a white candle in the figure of a dolphin
With a tiny flame spurting out of its groin
As it twirls in the night sky.
A sneeze of light in a dark hole.
A throw of dice in a chancy city.

I completely forgot to bring Frank a card.
Complete blank. Such thoughtlessness –
In my book – is a mortal sin.
The worst thing about loneliness
Is not loneliness.
The worst thing about loneliness
Is selfishness:
The savagery of selfishness.

# VIII

'Paul, is it time to draw the curtains?'
'If you say so, Frank.'
'Shopping for curtains, Paul.
Nothing like shopping for curtains.
Except for making love standing up
Shopping for curtains is the *crème de la crème*.
Shopping for curtains
In the curtains department
Of Byrne's in the Coombe.
The curtains saleswoman says:
"Well, sir, now, it all depends
On what you want from your curtains:
A highlight of your interior décor
Or to keep the cold night out?"
Deep stuff, curtains, deep stuff.'
He draws the curtains over Terenure,
Kimmage, Templeogue, the *Sunday World*.
I try to picture him
Making love standing up.
'Frank, do you mind me asking
What is it like –
Making love standing up?'
'I don't mind at all, Paul.
Well, actually, it was when
I was shopping for curtains.
I sat up on the counter
Swinging my legs absent-mindedly
While she was showing me her curtains.
But she got it into her head
That I was swinging my legs at her.

She came up and stood beside me.
She said that there was no one else
Around in the curtains department –
That it was a dead slack day.
She blinked her eyes.
She told me to stand down on my feet.
When I didn't cotton on
She lifted up my right leg
And tied it round her waist.
Then it dawned on me.
The 10p dropped.
She jumped up on the counter
And put her legs around me
And when I said to her
"I'm not a knee-trembling expert"
She said "Not to worry".
I made love to her standing up
As if I'd been doing it all my life.
She said that she hadn't felt like this
Since her first visit to the Giant's Causeway
After the start of the Peace Process.
She was the salt of the earth.
Not like your haughty housewife
Who over her potted plants
Waving her video zapper at you
Sniffs at love.
She said that I'd curtains on the brain
And that she hoped I'd come again.
She recommended deep dark red
Curtains – velours material.
I got yards of it off her.'
'Excellent Frank, but there's a lot

To be said also
For making love lying down
On your back.
Why do computer programmers always answer
When asked in questionnaires
In Sunday newspapers
What is your idea of Heaven? –
Snorkelling in Acapulco.
Why do they never say
What I would say?
My idea of Heaven as a man
Is to be lying on my back
Smiling up into the eyes of a woman,
Her face latticed by her hair,
Her shoulders braced
As she squats in her starting blocks.
She leaps out of her blocks
To race 100 metres
Over low hurdles
In 10.8 seconds
While I lie under her
Clinging to her
And she spits on my shoulder –
There! –
And whinnies and dozes
And then she straightens the pillows
And the blankets, folds me up,
All my parts,
And puts me away in her violin case
Until the next time she decides
To go to hounds and cross over the river
To the other side.'

Frank peers at me over his spectacles,
That baroque look of pained quizzicality:
'Paul, do you know
The Mammals of Mesopotamia?'
He smiles and I smile and I sigh
'I know them well, and
All belonging to them.
The Mammals of Mesopotamia –
They all went to school in St Columba's.'

## IX

It is five in the afternoon.
He switches off the television.
We listen – at my instigation –
To a fifteen-minute programme on the wireless
Advertised in the *Guide*
As the true story behind Robert Frost's poem
'Stopping by Woods on a Snowy Evening'.
We raise our eyebrows, purse our lips,
Shake our heads. No, sir, no.
The poem is the true story.
The true story is a lie.
Did it really happen?
If it was fictional, it happened.
Only the fictional is real.
Only the silken
Tent is real.
Only the bumble bee.
'At your instigation, Paul.'
'At my instigation, Frank.'
'And miles to go before I sleep . . .'
We yawn. We look at our watches.
'Frank, do you believe in the Annunciation?'
'I do, Paul, do you?'
'I do, Frank, and the sensational thing about it –
And I have only begun to realize this
Since receiving from Father Pat O'Brien of Skehanna
A haiku poem of his own making for Christmas
In which Mary says to the Angel Gabriel
Yes I will Yes I will yes yes yes –
For Christ's sake, Frank, the Annunciation

Is the ultimate yes-saying to life.
Mary leaves Molly Bloom sitting up in bed.
Mary leaves Zorba the Greek standing
And I love Zorba – I love Zorba more
Even than Judge O'Higgins of Stepaside
And, by Christ, as you and I know,
No one – forgive me for raising my voice
And getting excited, we have had such a peaceful
And at-ease-with-ourselves Christmas Day,
But the womanloneliness is beginning to get to
      me, Frank –
No one loves Zorba the Greek
Like Judge O'Higgins of Stepaside
Loves Zorba the Greek . . .
Nothing is as beautiful
As the virgin with child
Except the old man announcing her
On the piazza of St Mark;
His small, high, wizened voice,
His reedy cords,
Trembling on the waters
Of the canals of Venice;
Angelo the patriarch;
*Ave Maria, gratia plena:*
*Dominus tecum:*
*Benedicta tu in mulieribus.'*

'It's okay, Paul, it's okay, be emotional.
Women are God's chosen creatures. I agree.
First of all. Last of all.
*In mulieribus.*
Chief among them, Mary.

Especially the women who like Mary
Put no price on affection.
The women who simply like you for the clown
        that you are.
Who simply adore you for the clown that you are,
Who stay true to you for the clown that you are.
Last night – I mean the night before Christmas Eve –
In the hardware shop searching for a roasting tin –
I had to get a roasting tin especially for you, Paul –
I bumped into Joe and Marian stocking up in fuses.
I don't know my amps from my watts, do you, Paul?
Joe and Marian have been married thirty years
And they are still an item – still a courting couple.
Still talking about it. Hinting at it. Doing it.
Marian says to Joe in front of me in the hardware
        shop:
Thirty years ago Joe and I
Liked doing it best in the phone box at the bottom of
        Bath Avenue.
Joe purrs, more than one nostril hair significantly
        visible,
The privileged swine.
I agree with you, Paul, I agree with you.
Women are God's chosen creatures. I agree.
The Annunciation is a fantastic conception.
Like Television – the Annunciation is.
It makes neighbours of us all.
Rwanda. Tyneside. Mayo.
But – don't get me wrong, Paul,
Don't get me wrong –
Christmas Day is not as good as Good Friday.
Which would you prefer to be able to say:

Happy Christmas or Good Friday?
On Christmas Day man is born
But on Good Friday
Man goes one better – man dies
For his woman!
The ethical kiss!
Christmas Day is Happy
But Good Friday is Good.
Where were you born, Paul?'
'The Stella Maris.'
'On Earlsfort Terrace?'
'On Earlsfort Terrace.'
'Where will you die, Paul?'
'On the street.'
'Which street?'
'Dame Street.'
'Dame Street?'
'Outside Books Upstairs.'
'Under the eye of Ruth?'
'Under the eye of Ruth.'
'And Caroline?'
'And Caroline.'

X

We look at our watches again. Yawn again.
I look over at Frank, weighing up the odds.
Frank looks back over at me, weighing up the odds.
'Paul, you look like a man
In the dock at the Last Judgement!'
'That's how it always is, Frank,
At five in the afternoon
On Christmas Day.
*A las cinco de la tarde.*
A low-key duel in the waiting room
Of a provincial railway station.
To the jugular,
The judge is addicted.
God – a short lean matador
In a baseball cap – says:
"Okay, what did you do with your life?"
I say: "I made love."
He takes down his toothpick from his ear,
Inserts it between his teeth, chews it.
He turns to his computer, taps in,
Calls up all the women in my life,
Turns back to me again:
"You made what?"
"I made love."
"That's not what it says here."
Silence in the railway station.
All the buffers
Dripping with silence.
All the sleepers
Steaming with silence.

All the dumb metal.
God staring at me with open mouth,
Disbelief in his eyes.
The death-dealing swerve of the twentieth
    century
Is not that man stopped believing in God.
It's that woman stopped believing in man.
God spits out gristle.
There are no trains running.
Frank, do you think it would be possible
To watch a snatch of *High Society*?'
'I think that would be possible, Paul.
Which channel?' 'UTV'.
Grace Kelly and Bing Crosby are crooning
    'True Love'
Out in a yacht in the middle of the ocean.
Out in a yacht!
(Betimes in the kip I regret
My life as a stoat.
I wish I'd been a bit of a tycoon
With a yacht or two
Instead of an ould saint
With barely the price of the busfare.)
Frank sings along with them.
'How come you know this film by heart, Frank?'
'When I was a chiseller we had the record at home.'
Out here on the vein of a twig
In the forests of the suburbs of Dublin city,
Watching Frank singing 'High Society',
I surmise that in our own discreet way
He and I *are* High Society.

## XI

We look at our watches again. Yawn again.
Doorbell rings. 'That'll be him,' says Frank.
The Bowler – the man himself.
He lives out beyond in Glenageary –
In the Valley of the Sheep
Around the corner
From Godfrey.
On Christmas night he always
Drives over to collect Frank,
To bring Frank back out to Glenageary
For the night in order to ease
The passage into St Stephen's Day
And the Racing at Leopardstown –
The Annual Christmas Racing
Festival at Leopardstown.
The Bowler has brought a bottle of 'James
        Joyce' –
A non-alcoholic white wine.
Frank presents the Bowler with a Christmas
        present:
A Freedom Shaver With Gyroscopic Action
'Suitable' the logo says 'For Both Men & Women'.

I drag myself to my feet. 'Frank, I'll be away.
I am petrified of black ice on the roads.'
The Bowler – a lifelong driver –
Offers to drive ahead of me.
Wearily, warmly the Bowler smiles:
'I am an experienced sheep.'
He lets me drive in his slipstream

Back down to Ringsend.
I take his wheel,
Shelter in his slipstream all the way down
To Ringsend riding the black ice.

XII

Alone in my sheepfarm in Ringsend
On the banks of the freezing Liffey,
In my pen in Ringsend
With neighbours either side of me
And with my landlord in Westminster Downs
Whose lease stipulates
Tenants may not keep pets
Although my landlord herself
Is an arts administrator
And not only a woman
But a woman who keeps pets
And who has a husband
Who looks like a pet,
A small, bald man with a ponytail
Whose hobby is the IRA
In West Cork;
Who on a hot August Sunday afternoon
Through gritted teeth seethed to me:
Michael Collins was a womanizer!
I fooster for an hour or more
Not knowing what I am doing.
Glancing in mirrors.
Checking in mirrors.
Am I here?
Am I there?
Traipsing from room to room.
Taking down books.
Putting back books.
There are four rooms.
Twelve foot by twelve foot.

A dovecote of books with their beaks
In their spines – titles all bleached.
I take down *The Collected Poems of W. B. Yeats*
Which I knew by heart when I was fourteen
    years of age
And opening it at random at page 140 –
'The Cold Heaven' –
I discover a £20 note
Displaying the blue, horsey face of the poet,
All nostril and lip.
'Suddenly I saw a cold
And rook-delighting £20 note.'
The beauty of hiding money in books
Is that I can never remember
Which book I've hid it in.
I take down Steiner's *Heidegger*
To bring to bed with me:
'The secret king of thought'.
I take out my cache of Christmas cards,
Leaf through them for the umpteenth time.
(In the week before Christmas,
Day in, day out,
I have trembled to behold
My poor letterbox
With its bloated, scabby lips
Vomiting up Christmas cards.
My poor, demented
Barking-at-the-moon
Foaming-at-the-mouth letterbox.)
I spread out my cache on my mat.
Arrange them in batches
By size and subject,

Tenor and scope.
There is one card always that says:
Paul, you are not forgotten.
From a doctor in Zimbabwe.
My cache of Christmas cards
Will keep me going for six months
Until it is summer
And time to forget about last Christmas
And to think about next Christmas.
Summertime in Ringsend –
Christmas card-reading time.
I'll put them in a used Jiffy bag,
Fish them out
Every other week for a peek.
Waiting for the phone to ring
Knowing it won't ring.
It doesn't ring.
Once – about three weeks ago –
The phone rang.
It was for my daughter
Who is working in Mexico
Or Cuba – I'm not sure which.
Watching the telephone sit.
I kneel down at my bed,
Bury my head in my quilt,
Whisper my night prayers;
Rory of the Hills, pray for me –
I am a cretin;
Listen to reality's blowlamp
Roaring between my ears.
On the pinhead of contradiction
I juggle my despairs.

Stripped
In front of my daughter's mirror
I am not intimidated
By my ivy-wreathed body.
What am I
But a young girl myself
Before my looking glass
Pining for marriage?
At 10.30 p.m.
I stick myself into bed,
Read a page of Steiner's *Heidegger*,
Try on the driving gloves,
Put the Cockpit Kit under my pillow,
Counting myself to sleep.
Counting myself a lucky man
To be alive.
Intelligence, Memory, Orientation:
I am south of the river.
I remember New Zealand.
I can count to infinity.
Counting sheep.
I count Frank.
What is Frank doing now?

Watching the late-night movie on television
Or sitting on a small wall in Sicily
In his black hat and green socks,
In Erice westward-gazing to Ithaca,
Contemplating nightfall with a tender smile;
Archetypal petit-bourgeois Dubliner
Than whom there is no more rose-red
Spectacle in Central Asia or North Africa.

Aristocratic, modest, inspired.
All brow or no brow.
No newspapers. Only thrillers and prayerbooks.
A laconic messiah who scorns do-goodery
And hands over in cash half his wages to charity.
A rags-to-riches story.

# XIII

I was in Meath when you phoned at 8.30 a.m.:
'Paul, will you meet me in Dublin at 10.45
Outside the Carmelite Church in Beaumont –
Around the corner from Beaumont Hospital?'

In the early morning fog I drove across country,
The hills of East Meath and North Dublin,
By way of the Bolies and Stamullen,
The Naul and the Bog of the Ring.

Although I tried to guess why you had phoned
– Had you been sentenced to death by a doctor?
– Had you decided to marry or to become a monk?
– Had you decided to resign?

I did not pry, being grateful to you
For waking me, for being the cause
Of my driving along empty roads
In the heat haze of a May morning.

Crossroads after empty crossroads.
No signposts. No traffic signs.
Queen Anne's Lace, furze, white
Blossom of blackthorn in fog.

I could not see the tops of the hills
Of Bellewstown and Fourknocks.
I'd slept badly but now I felt well.
Filling up with the right kind of emptiness.

I hoped I'd be able to find the church in time.
I knew where Beaumont Hospital was –
Having been visiting Colm Tóibín at Christmas:
His circles of friends feasting at his well.

Buckets of time! I pulled in to the large
Carpark of the Church of the Nativity of Our Lord
At 10.40 and as I scanned the other parked cars
I saw you stand up the far side of the carpark.

You circled round my car. Leaning up against it,
Your hands on the roof over the passenger door,
You said: 'I've decided to put my head under
        the water.
I want to get baptized – rightly this time.'

I stare down at the ground – pebbles, grass
And – one solitary marigold
Wearing its heart on its tongue – its wet, orange
        tongue.
I mutter: 'Good man yourself.'

I glance up at you –
Odd man out.
I kick a pebble, staring at the one solitary marigold.
Jesus Christ!

You say that friends have chided you
For your habit of saying 'God bless'.
Henceforth you will be able to say with authority
'God bless'.

You are edgy before the ceremony at eleven.
You whisper: 'I want to pee.' I point out a tree
At a discreet distance from the adjacent primary
     school.
You step off into the trees at the far end of the church.

The priest comes out a door, shakes hands, smiles:
'Let's be about our business.'
We sit in a tiny oratory with five sanctuary lamps.
He puts on a white stole over pullover and slacks.

The priest hands me his copy of the Jerusalem Bible.
In my trembling witness's 'speaking-in-public voice'
I read from the Gospel of St John, Chapter 3:
The Conversation with Nicodemus.

'Not to judge the world
But so that through him the world might be saved.
No one who believes in him will be judged;
But whosoever does not believe is judged already.'

Words that scandalize.
I discover that conscience is the courage to improvise.
When the priest asks you to repeat 'Holy Catholic
     Church'
You change it to 'Holy Catholic *Christian* Church'.

Driving back to Drogheda – to the Tropical
     Medicine Unit
Of Our Lady of Lourdes Hospital –
I am to be vaccinated against Yellow Fever
Before my tour of Brazil –

I stop at the Ivory Coast pub in Balbriggan
For a bottle of mineral water.
I glimpse your sockets pop open beneath your bowed
    skull
Casting a warm eye on death.

Late last night reading the racing pages
You saw that in the 2.45 at Nottingham today
Christian Flight is 20 to 1.
Your life is a form of risk. What do you do?

If you were to go through with your baptism and back
    Christian Flight
She would not win!
So what you had to do is to go through with your
    baptism
And not back Christian Flight!

'CHRISTIAN FLIGHT SURPRISES' is the
    headline
In next day's newspaper.
Your dedication to chance as the ethic of fate;
Self-denial, humility, intuition.

'Christian Flight completed a rags-to-riches story
With a success in the Bradmore Fillies' Handicap at
    Nottingham yesterday.
The six-year-old battled to a neck victory
Over Le Bal at odds of 20 to 1.'

## XIV

I decide not to switch off the bedside light,
A white anglepoise from the Duty Free in Rome.
Thing I have never told Frank,
Have never told anyone.
For four-and-a-half years –
1984 to 1988 –
I had a girlfriend in Rome,
A West African nun.
The last time I saw her
At the Departure Gates in Rome Airport
She gave me a gift of the anglepoise,
The white anglepoise
With a screw-in bulb.
It was the first time in my life
I had seen a screw-in bulb.
It was typical of her.
She liked me, she said,
Because I looked studious.
A modern woman, par excellence.
It was her way of saying goodbye –
The white anglepoise;
Of ending our affair.
Like so many nuns
She was an out-and-out radical,
Yet modest and shy.
We met in St Peter's Square
At a papal audience.
I'd sat in her chair
By mistake. We started talking.
She had a car – a Fiat Uno.

We went walking
On the Janiculo.
For the next four-and-a-half years
Every three months
I went on pilgrimage to Rome.
I slept in the guest room in the convent.
I was apprehensive but she was adamant
That it made much more sense
Than staying in the hotel
In the Campo dei Fiori.
Either I'd sleep in her bed
Or she'd sleep in my bed.
All she was interested in
Was making love;
Sparking off one another;
Whisking the daylights out of each other.
She didn't want to see me
Except to make love to me.
I don't think she felt
That I was her intellectual equal.
Her days were spent in
Theological exploration –
She said – to determine
If man is divine
Or human solely.
I shut my eyes
Opening them only to stare
At the dumb telephone
Growing dumber as the waters of the Liffey
Scrape their knives under my window.
The receiver in its cradle
Is limp as a tot asleep

Face down in its cot.
I blink at the receiver
With pity and tenderness.
The art of blinking
Is not hard to master.
*Improvise. Improvise.*
I enjoy blinking.
Just as when I was a teenager
I excelled at jiving
At the hop above the shop
And I was not averse to showing off
My jive technique
I excel at blinking.
I like to blink.
I like to blink and blink and blink and blink
To make you think
I do not think
I know what I think.
I think I know what I think.
I think I think I blink.
I could have had Grace Kelly for my wife
If I had not blinked.
Instead on a breezy day
In Westport, on the side
Of a mountain, feeling
Guilty about my family,
I blinked, and Grace Kelly
Flew off back to Monaco
With her monastic spouse,
Prince Rainier.
I sailed my soul in the sea
Of Clew Bay.

Eyed by jellyfish.
Fingered by seaweed.
The thing I am afraid of
Is of dying alone
In a home in Bray
With Alzheimer's disease
After ten years
Of meals on wheels –
Yet in my bed alone tonight
I am not afraid.
I am floating above my bed
Peering down at myself:
No longer a prisoner
Of my father and mother;
I am a red balloon
High up in my own white ceiling;
One of Frank's balloons;
If only tonight for a few minutes
Replete with emptiness,
The right kind of emptiness;
Not a burst balloon
To be scraped off her thigh
By a woman for whom
Her man is a fine mess.
I am a balloon full of air,
Full of emptiness,
Drifting across my own ceiling,
The Ontario of my soul
Far down below me
In the Dublin of my body.

*

All St Stephen's Day
The telephone stays asleep
Until the day after St Stephen's Day
When Frank telephones me at 10.30 a.m.:
'I had coffee and crispies
Sitting opposite a civil servant from Dolphin's Barn.
She is going away to the Andes
With the Friends of Kew Gardens.'


*No longer are you to be named 'Forsaken',*
*nor your land 'Abandoned',*
*but you shall be called 'My Delight'*
*and your land 'The Wedded'.*

# A GOOSE
# IN THE FROST

*To Seamus Heaney in Stockholm, December 1995*

In the goose house at night the geese
Scour the walls where the walls meet the floors
For the darkest wainscot; nothing less
Than the darkest wainscot – the darkest deepdown
    wainscot – will do.
*Darkness is all. Geese go by the light.*

Out of the Caspian Sea the sun is ladder-
    rattling west
Over the Caucasus, daubing the highlands
Of Armenia with undercoat;
Pebbledashing the Crimea;
Twirling its paintbrush in the fog on the Black Sea;

Dragging its horsehair across the Mediterranean;
Gonging the Aegean; xylophoning the Carpathians;
Trumpeting the Alpes Maritimes in a livid lather.
As shepherds in the Pyrenees – Magi of
    Transhumance –
Are plucking at the earlobes of their snoozing
    spouses –

*Encore de la jour* in which to be articulate,
To be rhetorical about sheep's udders,
Wool, and the first *cafés au lait* of the day
Are being brewed in Toulouse and Tarbes –
In the dead silence of first light in Derry

Geese are waking up keening with desire.
The goose house is a monastery
Teeming with tantalizing women
Drifting about in the darkness.
*Darkness is all. Geese go by the light.*

The shit of ten thousand predecessors
Is the satiny mattress upon which bubble
Spools of goosely desire:
Stirrings in Derry in 1995
Procreate a thirtieth-century Armenian goose.

They are shuffling their feathers to order;
Bump to the goose house door to queue up
For the light – to queue up and to peel off
At the altar rail of the half-door when the bolt
Is yanked back; goose, gander, gosling –

In that order – file out, turn right,
Trundle down aisle between nettle stalks of
    Childhood;
Straight on out under the arch of Adolescence;
Left along the gauntlet to the weeping willow of
    Adulthood;
Right through the wrought-iron garden gate

Into the Front Garden of Infancy.
What are we? Vehicles of memory,
Long memory, capacious with curiosity;
Queue-maestros in file swaying along skylines;
Males oozing at our orifices with hegemony;

Airbuses zigzagging across ocean floors.
Grass. At last. First, light; secondly, grass.
A passion for grass. But this daybreak –
Frost. White host
Focusing out of gold monstrance of sunrise.

God with his mother's milk in a spiky halo.
Am I in the correct crèche? The correct oratory?
Whatever I had made allowance for,
I had not made allowance for this.
What kind of oasis is an oasis with no grass?

What is this nuptial froth that the priests
        call frost?
This pabulum that weighs so ponderously
On the souls of snowdrops?
Oh, and indeed, and aye, I make a wee bit of
        a fuss;
A wee bit of a rumpus.

I throb, shudder, squawk; flap
My wings; stump about my spouse;
Gossip to my goslings but almost
Instantly slide out of my kneeler
To roost in God's semen,

The eucharistic seed.
I sink down deep into frost
With my fury in my breast;
Rock with exuberance in it;
I who never lusted after frost

Nor had beak know-how of frost;
Who navigated only for grass –
Smooth-stalked grass geese dream of –
See myself at sea in the frost;
A goose in the frost

The day the earth stands still:
A goose is a flying saucer beached
In a white field circled by Magi;
A goose – to look you in the eye –
Squints slant.

The end of poetry is innocence:
A child in the sun;
One who knows how to take his time.
My project is to be placid which I am.
Wherefore I disintegrate with rectitude in the
        rising sun.

Fore and aft in frost
I lean out over the prow of my soul;
Focus my prehistoric eyes;
Dip my beak in particulars;
Suck crystals; daydream

A goose I knew,
The goldenest goose in goosedom,
Who asphyxiated of loneliness
In a basement room
In St Stephen's Green;

Who is interred
In a common grave
In Glasnevin
Under lager cans, used condoms;
Who is gesticulating to me

From the shore like a goose girl
With his dog-collar round her wrist
Waving to the conscience-chasmed priest
Upon the waters of Goldengrove,
A neck in a punt.

*He in the treetops, a drowned man spinning,*
*Beholds her green eyes bloom;*
*A goose girl in her fourteenth year*
*Be the snowdrop of Elysium;*
*Let my ego die.*

*Harry, Deirdre, John, Christiane*
*Feeding crumbs to the geese;*
*Circling the soul of Father Hopkins;*
*The star-struck loneliness of man.*
*Afternoon tea in the Shelbourne.*

Goose girl – goodbye,
Teach me to see.
How to sow my vow.
How to die.
How to say Goodbye

With a smile on my beak.
How not to cry
As with gauche élan
Wolves circle my soul.
*Darkness is all. Geese go by the light.*


*Hotel Wales, Madison Avenue, New York/*
*La Louveterie, Puyvert, Vaucluse*

# NOTES

12  *Ad deum qui laetificat juventutem meam*:
To God, who gives joy to my youth.

13  *Bonjour, mon père*: Good day, Father.

58  *Ave Maria, gratia plena: / Dominus tecum: /
Benedicta tu in mulieribus*:
Hail Mary, full of grace: / the Lord is with thee: /
Blessed art thou amongst women.

61  *A las cinco de la tarde*: At five in the afternoon;
the refrain from the opening section of Lorca's
'Lament for Ignacio Sanchez Mejias'.